CONSTRUCTING YOUR NEW HOME with a BUILDER

The definitive step by step process explained...that will save you time and money!

BRYAN CANAVAN

CONSTRUCTING YOUR NEW HOME WITH A BUILDER

ISBN (paperback): 978-0-646-81052-2

Book design by www.DominiDragoone.com
Cover photos by Delior Manli/iStock and Pgiam/iStock

All photographs in this book have been sourced from Canva Stock Images, except: The following photographs / images have been sourced via courtesy Stroud Homes Brisbane South: Page 1 – Tom Eldridge; Page 21 – Contour surveys x 2; Page 23 – Cut and fill graphs x 2; Page 24 – Internal stairs x 2; Page 29 – Waffle pod spacer; Page 45 – Effluent Spray and HSTP tank; Page 46 – Concrete water tanks; Page 61 – Driveway crossover; Page 66, Author self image, sourced from private collection.

Contact the author at:
bcanavan@bigpond.net.au
www.facebook.com/people/Bryan-Canavan

Printed in Australia.

To assist new home buyers with their budgeting, numerous examples are given, pointing out approximate costings to be expected.

It should be noted the book was compiled in 2019 and pricing will change over time, probably in line with the Consumer Price Index in Australia.

While the book has been written from within the Queensland market, the principles will remain the same for all Australian states and territories, even though some of the terminology may differ in some examples.

Contents

PART III

STROUD
HOMES
Feels like home

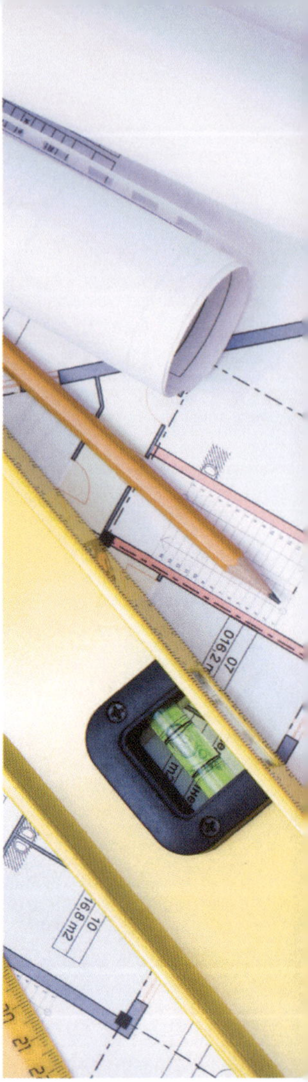

Foreword

Over the past six years I have had the pleasure of working closely with Bryan Canavan. Each and every home that I've been involved in building over that time (somewhere around 400 homes) has been sold by Bryan, and the most enjoyable part of building those homes has been seeing them change along with the industry and along with the knowledge gained by our entire team.

We have adapted our product at Stroud Homes and have been able to give our clients the best available product on the market every year. The building industry is one that constantly gains in complexity as technology improves. Bryan has spent his entire career improving his knowledge of the industry and has taken the time to summarise that experience in this short book for your benefit.

Make sure to take notice of all aspects in this book; it will literally save you thousands, and more importantly, save you a lot of emotional stress that comes with inexperience.

Once you know what to expect and how to approach a build, it is one of the most enjoyable and exciting things that you will take on in life.

Enjoy the read and your upcoming build!

—Tom Eldridge, Director and Licensed Builder,
Stroud Homes Brisbane South

Introduction

CONSTRUCTING YOUR NEW HOME WITH A BUILDER

This book is designed to assist anyone who is thinking about building a new home. Even if you have never built before, I'm sure you will take something out of it that will assist you in the process of building your new home and should even save you time and money.

It is mainly written based on the questions from the 440 plus clients I have helped bring their new home dreams to reality over the past seven years. It is also based on the personal experience gained from the six new homes my wife and I have built over the past 40 years.

Boy – did we make some mistakes! I wish I'd had a book like this before we built our first home at the tender age of 21 on the Gold Coast.

The book has intentionally been written on a non-technical basis. I have intended it to be easy and quick to read and understand. I hope you find it readable and informative.

To this end, you will see bullet point facts set out to impart some knowledge on each phase of the journey in a simple format.

A glance over the contents will show you that the guide is in chronological order, so you don't have to get too far ahead of yourself. But I would encourage you to read through it once, and it will be easy to come back and refresh the category you are up to yourself.

Best of luck with your construction journey. By following the listed processes here, you won't need luck to have a successful outcome!

—Bryan Canavan

PART I

The Construction Process

THE JOURNEY BEGINS

First, you must make a decision:

- Buy an existing home, or,
- Build a new one

Next, there are three main components to be considered:

- Land
- Design
- Builder

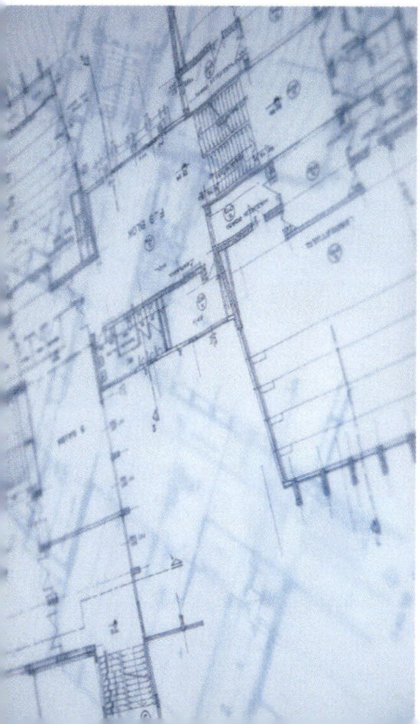

Fact Sheet

Old versus New

THE JOURNEY BEGINS

Do you just buy an existing home or build a new one? This is a topic that has been passionately debated over the years, at Sunday BBQs and across the dinner table. To be fair, both options have their "good" and "not so good" points.

Apart from the six brand new homes I've built over the years, I've also bought and renovated four old/existing homes, with the oldest being a charming (but terribly run down) home built in 1866!

Putting all these experiences together, I would recommend building new every time. The reasons for this are listed below.

Here are the Pros and Cons on Building a New Home:

PROS

- **No stamp duty** is paid on the new home which means a huge saving! You only pay stamp duty on the land – saving thousands of dollars (refer to the Stamp Duty overview).
- You can pick a **plan that suits you** and your family, today and for the future. A good builder will also allow you to customise your design to suit your own needs.
- This means you are not buying someone else's plan. Yes – you can make changes to an existing home, but there goes more time and money.
- Energy efficiency: new homes go through a high level of energy testing, including a 6-star energy rating, meaning **your energy costs will be far less.**
- You get to **choose the inclusions** and **select colours** to suit your own taste and existing furniture.

- **New warranties** on all inclusions, from tiles to taps. You will also have a seven-year structural warranty and a 25-year guarantee on the frame.
- This means **greatly reduced maintenance** on your home because everything is new.
- Get that **"new car"** feeling throughout the entire home.

CONS

- **Construction time:** you are looking at around six to eight months before you are in your new home. This will vary greatly by builder, check the builders guaranteed construction time before committing. (this time period **includes your planning time and council approval time**).
- While you are building, you will need **alternative accommodation**; e.g. rent, or move in with Mum!

Fact Sheet

Land

THE JOURNEY BEGINS

For the purpose of this exercise, we will view land as falling into one of two categories:

Residential land – this is typically land that a developer has established into an estate, and broadly speaking, each block will be from 300m2 to 800m2. I, my mother and my grandmother were brought up on a typical quarter acre block (1,000m2), but this size block is now considered to be small acreage. Residential land will be serviced by town sewerage and full pressure town water. It will usually be fairly flat and ready to build on.

Acreage land – this is land from around 1,000m2 to 2-5 acres (8,000m2 to 20,000m2) These blocks can be developed as part of an acreage estate or can be old blocks that may have been used for farming in the past, but demand is causing them to be sold off as acreage housing land. The one-off blocks can be very large, up to 20 acres and above.

- There is good demand for acreage land as a lot of people do not want to be close enough to touch their neighbours, and the fact that supply of acreage is running out means it will be a good investment in the years to follow.
- While some acreage land won't be that much more expensive to purchase than an average residential block, there are additional costs involved in building on acreage land that can quickly suck up your budget. So do look into the full picture before signing up.

We'll cover all these topics in detail later, but some of the possible additional costs that come with acreage land are:

- **Cut and fill –** typically $3,500 extra.
- **Home sewerage treatment plant (HSTP) –** typically $11,000 (*around 95% of acreage blocks* <u>*do not*</u> *have town sewerage and will require a HSTP*).
- **Water tanks –** typically $15,000 for concrete, in ground water tanks with a pump (*most of the newer acreage estates* <u>*do have*</u> *full pressure town water now*).
- **Retaining walls –** from $10,000 to $60,000.
- **Rock mitigation –** from $3,000 to $20,000 (*average of around $6,000*).
- **Bushfire mitigation –** from $3,500 to $30,000 (*average of around $5,000*).
- **Acoustic mitigation –** from $2,000 to $5,000.
- **Tree removal –** typically $1,500.
- **Driveway –** will vary greatly, depending how far back you set your home (*average of around $6,000 for plain concrete*).
- **Services –** this covers power, power pole, water and stormwater and will vary greatly depending on the block size and home positioning (average is less than $1,000 all up but can run to $60,000 on very large blocks).

Bear in mind that some of the above costs can apply to residential land as well, but usually it will not be as expensive as the costs noted here.

I certainly do not want to scare you off acreage land, but simply want you to be informed on what can be around the corner. I will go so far as to say that I have never seen all the above apply to the one block; the total average in additional costs to build on acreage land is around $20,000 to $25,000.

What to look for when considering residential or acreage land:

- **Contours –** general slope or fall on the block, especially where you plan to build your home on that block.
- **Orientation –** which way the block is facing, especially the western sun – you do not want this hitting your alfresco and living areas directly.
- **Price –** cheapest is not always the best! If you must add $20,000 to $40,000 of the above items to build your home, the block is not that cheap, is it?
- **Drainage –** how well does the land drain? Can it be easily controlled after the cut and fill? It's very important to keep water away from the slab.
- **Rock/bushfire/acoustic mitigation –** will this be needed?
- **Services –** is power, water, NBN included or can they be easily connected?

Fact Sheet

Design

THE JOURNEY BEGINS

These days, most builders have a good range of standard plans, anything from 25 to 125 plans. You can usually find a plan that either suits you perfectly, or with some modification, will be just right. However, be aware that some builders won't allow changes to their plans, so check this before getting involved with them. Also, some builders will charge you for this service – again, check on this first.

Managing design costs – most people will usually want more than their budget will allow. We are all like that when starting to look at making a major purchase. This can be anything from buying the latest big screen TV to a new car and certainly, buying a new home.

There's nothing wrong with that – but for the purchase to proceed, there will need to be a compromise somewhere. Firstly, make a list of what you want in a new home and what you actually need in a new home. There is a big difference between the two. Get your "need" list satisfied first, then see what can be added from your "want" list.

But it's my forever home! If I had a dollar for every time I've heard that, I'd be sitting on the beach in the West Indies right now! I do accept that, in about 5-10% of cases, this will be the outcome, but if you cannot squeeze that jacuzzi into this home, try next time!

I'm over budget! Ok, that is fine and completely normal, I have rarely delivered a quote to one of my clients and heard "Wow, that's great, it's under my budget". Here are the quick and simple ways to reduce your costs and still get a brand new home:

- **Area –** Reduce the total area of the home. You don't have to delete the media room but try taking a little off most rooms; you'll be surprised what you will save. As a very rough average, for every square metre you can reduce, you will save around $1,000. So, if you can find 10m2, there's around $10,000 off the total!
- **Façade –** your home's façade can be a budget killer. A good looking and inexpensive façade will be mainly brick with a feature of cladding. A good builder will be able to show you how attractive this looks when managed correctly, including co-ordinating colours. Potential savings from cutting out the fancy façades with render, stonework, raised and exposed timber gables, etc, can be from $10,000 to $35,000.
- **Inclusions –** Have you added a lot of upgrades? Re-visit them and see how much you will save; e.g., exposed aggregate for the driveway is about 40% more expensive than standard concrete. Also, consider what can be added later without a lot of hassle. In six to twelve months' time, chances are you will be financially better off. Things like the driveway, pool, solar PV system etc, can all be added later.

So, these are the three main areas you should visit first, if you're trying to squeeze into that budget and still have a brand new home for the family and yourself.

Fact Sheet

Builder

THE JOURNEY BEGINS

This is one of your major decisions, as once you sign a contract with your builder, you are generally stuck with them – for better or for worse! Having worked in the home building industry for around seven years, I've heard a lot of stories about builders; some would make your hair curl!

The purpose of this segment is not to name and shame any builder, but to give you some tips on how to recognise what you can expect from that builder during the course of your new home being built.

If you see any of these characteristics during your early contact with your potential builder – ***RUN!***

- **Absolutely gorgeous display home,** with all the trims, but the consultant can't (or won't) tell you how much the standard home costs; guaranteed there's some wool being pulled over your eyes here.
- **Home price given seems really cheap –** be a little sceptical at this point. Ask if the price includes the applicable site cost items; and does the price include all inclusions? Long after the price is delivered and forgotten – service remains!
- **Is this a fixed price quote?** Even if the consultant says it is, ask for it to be stated in writing that the price won't change if you sign a contract.
- **Is this a fixed price contract? –** even more important than above, it must be in writing that you are signing a fixed price contract.
- **Do your homework –** you are considering entering a contract with this builder for probably the biggest investment you have made in your life so far, so due diligence is warranted.

Check on the following areas – apart from anything, they will be a direct pointer to the level of customer service offered:

- **Search productreview.com.au** – what is the builder's star rating out of five? What are the client's comments/complaints? Every builder will have some client not 100% happy. Read the builder's plan of action on how he plans to address the client's concerns.
- **Local Facebook pages** – most local estates/areas have community Facebook pages; join up and look at any feedback.
- **Testimonials** – ask the builder for testimonials from his clients. It is unlikely you will get bad ones, but you can usually tell quickly if they are genuine.
- **Contact the QBBC** (Qld Building and Construction Commission – other states will have a similar industry body that issues builders' licences) and complete a licence check: is the builder licenced? How many strikes against the builder, how many remain unresolved?

Communication – building a new home can be emotional at times. You need to have confidence in your chosen builder that you can talk to them directly, to resolve anything that may come up.

Compare apples with apples – when looking at two or three builders' quotes, it's very hard to make a true comparison because each builder will structure their pricing differently. For example, some run low starting prices but offer very low inclusions; you need to make sure you check off exactly what's being offered. Watch the quality of the inclusion also; a lot of builders will run "builders' brands" appliances which will be about half the price but half the quality of a recognised brand.

Marketing offers – try and use common sense here. It's understandable a builder will have a special offer from time to time; e.g, maybe a free upgrade to stone benchtops, but when you see a builder offering $50,000 worth of "free" upgrades for a $5,000 payment… something isn't right. They will have jacked the starting price up to cover part of the promotional cost and usually give you a book that you can choose your upgrades from, at heavily inflated prices (sometimes two and even three times the normal price, meaning your $50,000 is only worth about $15,000). Trust me – there are numerous builders – and well-known national builders – who do this.

Member of industry associations – check if the builder is a member of reputable and recognised member associations; e.g., in Queensland:

- QMBA – Queensland Master Builders Association.
- HIA – Housing Industry of Australia.

Build time – does the builder offer a guaranteed built time and an actual date that handover will take place? Does this form part of your contract with the builder? Are liquidated damages paid to you by the builder if they fail to achieve this date?

PART II

The Construction Process

PLAN, DECIDE, ACTION

Typically, the plan, decide, & action part of the construction process will take 3 to 4 months. Let's look at the planning process in a simple step by step flow chart:

START HERE!

Allow 7 Days

- Talk to Mortgage Brokers/Banks: How much can I borrow?

Allow 21 Days

- Decide on your Area/Land
- Place a deposit on a block

Allow 21 Days

- **Decide on your Home Design**
- **Decide on your Builder**

Allow 14 Days

- **Sign an agreement with your Builder**
- **Complete Tests and Surveys on your Land**

Allow 7 Days

- **Finalise colour selections and inclusions**

Allow 7 Days

- **Sign a Building Contract (subject to finance, submit contracts to financier)**

Allow 14 Days

- **Finance Approval! (Builder to submit plans to council)**

Allow 21 Days

APPROVED COUNCIL PLANS!

Fact Sheet

QLD Stamp Duty

PLAN, DECIDE, ACTION

(Numbers will differ from State to State, check with your State Government for local details)

Stamp duty (now known as transfer duty) is essentially a tax on the transfer of property, payable to the government by the buyer of the property.

Who is liable to pay Stamp Duty?
The duty is paid by the purchaser; however, there are some concessions available, e.g., first home buyer.

Remember – when you build a new home, there is **NO STAMP DUTY** paid on the cost of ***building a new home*** – the only stamp duty to be paid is on the cost of the land.

If you are not sure, consult your financier or solicitor, as you need to know this up front; the dollars are very big here.

Don't forget, if you buy an **existing home,** you will pay stamp duty on the **total price!**

STAMP DUTY CALCULATOR

ESTABLISHED HOUSE AND LAND

Stamp Duty will vary for land and investment purchase.

For up-to-date figures check with your financial adviser. QLD rates provided.

PURCHASE PRICE	STAMP DUTY
$475,000	$7,875
$500,000	$8,750
$525,000	$9,625
$550,000	$10,600
$575,000	$11,725
$600,000	$12,850
$625,000	$13,975
$650,000	$15,100
$675,000	$16,225
$700,000	$17,350
$725,000	$18,475
$750,000	$19,600
$775,000	$20,725
$800,000	$21,850

STAMP DUTY CALCULATOR

LAND ONLY PURCHASE

Stamp Duty will vary for land and investment purchase.

For up-to-date figures check with your financial adviser. QLD rates provided.

PURCHASE PRICE	STAMP DUTY
$100,000	$1,000
$125,000	$1,250
$150,000	$1,500
$175,000	$1,750
$200,000	$2,000
$225,000	$2,250
$250,000	$2,500
$275,000	$2,750
$300,000	$3,000
$325,000	$3,250
$350,000	$3,500
$375,000	$4,375
$400,000	$5,250
$425,000	$6,125

Numbers accurate as of August 2019.

Fact Sheet

Site Costs

PLAN, DECIDE, ACTION

Site costs are the combination of various tasks that must be undertaken to prepare your block for the construction of your new home. The main components that make up site costs are:

- Soil type.
- Cut and fill.
- Presence of rock.
- Retaining walls.
- Trees to be removed.
- Spoil removal (only applicable to small lots).
- Zero lot boundary (only applicable to small lots).

Check and identify each specific site cost component that may be applicable to your block. It's important to do this ASAP, as they can singularly and collectively have a big impact on your budget.

Over the coming pages, we'll explore each of these components in more detail so you can be better prepared if they become an issue on your land. Identifying and pricing your site costs is a vital part of your new home consideration.

Fact Sheet

Site Works

PLAN, DECIDE, ACTION

Cut and fill – cutting and filling the natural ground for your new home pad may be required to provide a level and structurally stable foundation for the construction of your home.

The required cut and fill are determined via a contour survey of your land. At first glance, contour surveys can be confusing to read; see list below for an explanation of how to read your contour survey:

- No two contour lines can meet or cross each other
- Equally spaced contour lines indicate uniform slope
- The closer the contour lines are spaced the slope is steep
- The wider the contour lines are spaced the slope is gentle
- Contour lines are usually measured in 250mm to 1m increments

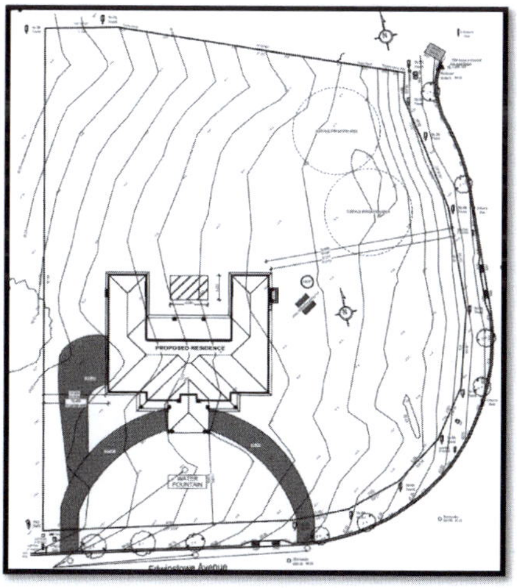

Example of a Contour Survey with house plan placed.

Retaining and batter - depending on the size of your land, as well as the severity of the cut and fill needed, you may require retaining walls.

Usually on acreage blocks the cut and fill can be battered, given the extra land area available. Battering is when the cut earth is gently sloped, taking the newly created level to natural ground level. If space allows, battering is always the best and most cost efficient option.

Examples of how a batter works on the cut side of a cut and fill block:

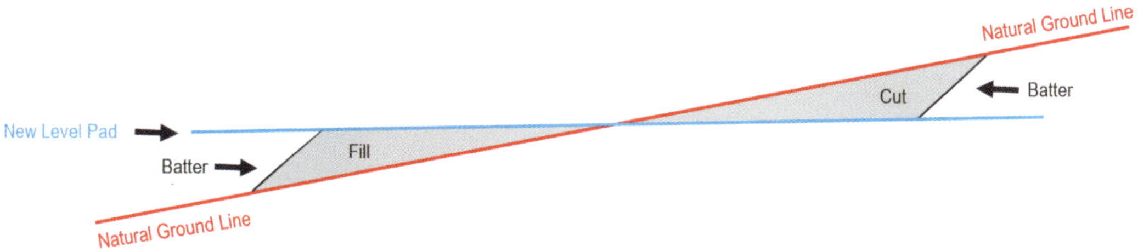

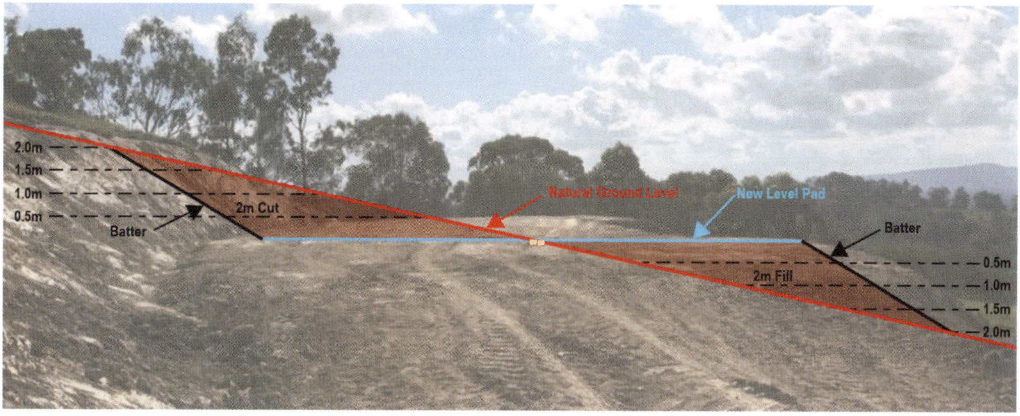

Blue line =

New level pad, your home's slab will be poured on this area.

Red line =

Simulates where the natural ground level was, prior to the cut and fill.

Black line =

The batter area; the cut area slopes upwards, the fill area slopes downwards.

Split level designs – If your land has an extreme slope (> four metres) or is a particularly difficult site, it may be an idea to consider a split level design. Most homes can be adapted to suit a split level design.

Keep in mind that these changes are more complex than a standard slab design, and there are some factors that need to be taken into consideration early in the design process.

Split level designs will also add to your costs, typically around $15,000 plus or minus, depending on the home and block.

Above: Internal stairs to the lower level
Right: Internal stairs to the upper level

Split level homes can offer a great solution that will be tailored directly to your specific block. Split level homes will typically have multiple staircases but only small ones, five to seven stairs on each. You will usually have two small staircases in your home, but there can be more depending on the contours of your land.

You would usually only consider a split level home if the fall on your block is in the high category. In this circumstance, this type of home is a very practical solution. If you are lucky enough to have views from your block, a split level home will take full advantage of them, as you're not cutting and filling your block to bring the whole home down to one low level.

There may be some other advantages in building a split level home:

- Reducing what would have been a very steep driveway from the road to your garage.
- Overcoming potential building height restrictions set by your council.
- Reducing the cut and fill amount required, saving money and avoiding huge retaining walls.

Fact Sheet

Soil Type

PLAN, DECIDE, ACTION

Why does soil type even matter?

The type of soil you are about to build your home on will determine the slab type needed. Please note that this is not at the discretion of the builder but is the responsibility of the structural engineer.

The earth under your construction is the foundation for your new home. It will have an impact on your home over its entire lifetime. It's important to have the soil tested and certified by professionals.

What is being tested in your soil?

In basic terms, the engineer will determine your soil's reaction (movement), to both extreme wet and dry conditions. Your soil is being tested to find out how it reacts to these conditions, and ultimately, the slab type designed by the structural engineer will be based on these results.

How is the test done?

Two to three bore holes are drilled into the surface of your block, in the area where your new home is to be built. The holes are only small (only around 80mm in diameter) and the augur bit will go down as deep as 4m. These core samples are then taken to the laboratory for testing. This process will produce a result in 10 to 14 days.

What do the soil classifications mean?

- Soil types with the classification of A, S, M, H1 and H2 have the typical specification of "nominal/standard waffle" pod design, from Australian Standards S2870. Each classification will require a different slab design, getting stronger the further you move down the scale of soil type classification.
- Soil types with the classification of E will see the engineer use a conventional stiffened raft slab within ground beams.
- Soil types with properties of P are looked at on a case by case basis, as no two sites will be the same. The engineer will also determine the need to have concrete piers set into the ground prior to pouring the slab.

What are the possible Soil Classifications?

A = Acceptable
S = Slightly Reactive
M = Moderately Reactive
H1 = Highly Reactive
H2 = Highly Reactive
E = Extreme
P = Particular (usually as a result of presence of trees on site or fill on site)

What type of slab will be required?

- As your soil type classification moves down the scale, the engineer will make each slab design stronger to withstand the expected movement on your block. They will use a slightly thicker slab, the concrete used will be a higher MPA (Mega Pascal, stress/strength of concrete), and thicker steel reinforcement is needed.

The soil type and subsequent slab determination is one of the most vital components of your build.

Fact Sheet

Waffle Pod Slabs

PLAN, DECIDE, ACTION

Waffle pod slabs are an innovative system utilised during the construction of concrete slabs for new residential homes, providing enormous strength and durability and significantly reducing building costs.

- The Institution of Engineers Australia awarded the waffle pod system with an Engineering Excellence Award.
- The system itself is designed to comply with Australian Quality Standard AS 2870-2011 Residential Slabs and Footings.
- ***Waffle pod slabs have been in Australia for 30 plus years!***

What are the benefits of a waffle pod slab?

- Waffle pod slabs can accurately predict the required concrete quantities.
- This means there is a reduction of waste and an increase in construction efficiency.
- There is minimal disturbance of soil.
- There is no need to pay for spoil removal from the site as there is no excavated matter from the trenches.

Are waffle pod slabs just as strong as conventional or raft slabs?

- Waffle pod slabs are stronger, as the slab is poured as one piece.
- A conventional slab has the footings and slab poured separately.
- Both slab types are equivalent in terms of stiffness and flexibility.
- Both slab types are 85mm to 110mm thick in concrete, as specified by the engineer, based on the soil type.
- Both slab types will have reinforced mesh, 8-9mm in diameter.

What are the advantages of using waffle pod slabs?

- Approximately 30% less expensive than conventional slabs, saving you money.
- Have more concrete beams and closer centres than conventional slabs, making them stronger.
- Use consistent spacers between the pod and mesh, giving greater balance and strength.
- Less susceptible to changing weather conditions.

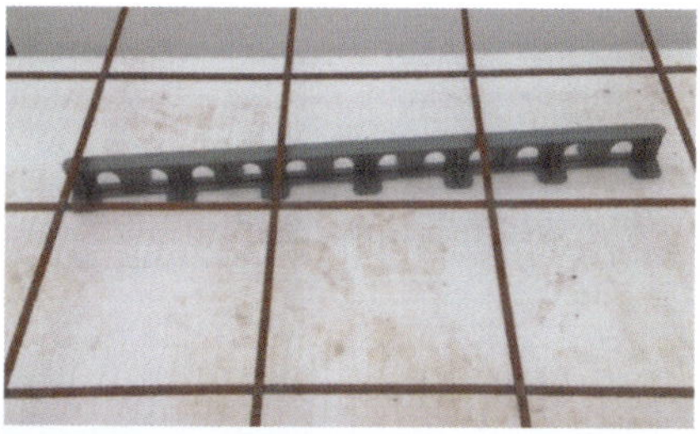

Fact Sheet

Bushfire Mitigation

PLAN, DECIDE, ACTION

The Building Code of Australia requires the construction of buildings in bushfire prone areas to follow the specific requirements of the Australian Standards: 3959. These building requirements for house designs and constructions vary according to the bushfire attack level (BAL) that a development and your block within that development fall into.

You should find out if your block is covered by a bushfire overlay; the seller of the land will normally provide this information. Alternatively, you can contact your local council to see if your block falls into a bushfire overlay zone.

If your block is in a **bushfire overlay zone**, you will require a site-specific **bushfire report** carried out by a **bushfire engineer**. Your builder can organise this or you can organise it yourself (cost will be from around $1,000). This is not an optional choice for you; it must be done to gain final approval on your home.

Here are the **Australian Standards** requirements to be completed by the builder for homes identified as being in a bushfire overlay zone, for the various BAL ratings:

BAL LOW

No additional building requirements for this rating level.

BAL 12.5

- Weephole in the brickwork is required to have a weephole protector that has a stainless steel mesh insert at the back of the weephole to stop embers from getting into the framework.
- All windows require 5mm toughened glazing, in lieu of 4mm standard glazing.

- Fly and security screens are required to have an aluminium wire, rather than a poly wire.
- Front door requires a fire resistant frame and upgraded door glazing to meet the requirements.
- Garage door requires fire resistant weather strips.
- Roof is required to be fully sarked and roof vents must have fire resistant weather strips.

BAL 19 and BAL 29

All inclusions required by the BAL 12.5 rating bushfire construction **plus** the following additions:

- Facia and gutters need to be fixed at 450mm centres in lieu of 600mm centres which will require extra noggins to be installed between the truss tails.
- Garage door requires a fire resistant frame.
- Front doors in this range are limited and may require an upgraded screen door.

BAL 40 to FZ (flame zone)

All inclusions required by the BAL 12.5, 19 and 29 rating bushfire construction **plus** the following additions:

- All windows require 6mm toughened glazing, in lieu of the standard 4mm glazing.
- Roof penetration requires stainless steel mesh inserted to prevent embers from entering.
- Eave sheeting needs to be 6mm thick, in lieu of standard 4.5mm.
- Fixed glass panels on sliding and stacker doors require screens across both doors.
- FZ rating may require bushfire shutters.

Bushfire Attack Level (BAL)	Distance from Threat
BAL – LOW	> 100m
BAL – 12.5	26m – < 100m
BAL – 19	18m – < 26m
BAL – 29	13m – < 18m
BAL – 40	11m – < 13m
BAL –Flame Zone	< 11m

The above individual BAL ratings are based on:

- The region where you live
- The type of vegetation around your property
- The distance from your home to individual vegetation types
- The slope on your property.

Fact Sheet

Acoustic Overlays (Noise Mitigation)

PLAN, DECIDE, ACTION

Objective

To ensure all habitable rooms in a relevant residential building are designed and constructed to adequately protect the occupant's health and safety from transport noise due to state controlled roads and local government roads and train lines.

Queensland Development Code (MP4.4)

The Queensland Development Code MP4-4 "Buildings in a Transport Noise Corridor" September 2010 (QDC) specifies noise categories to ensure that habitable rooms of residential buildings are adequately protected from transport noise.

When is acoustic mitigation usually required?

Typically, acoustic mitigation will be required when the dwelling is exposed to excessive noise levels. Some examples of this include:

- Proximity to busy roads and freeways
- In the flight path of aircraft
- Near train stations
- Exposure to factory noise.

Noise category/treatment required:

Category 0 – No additional acoustic treatment required.

Category 1 – Reduction of 25-35 decibels, applies to entry doors, external walls, roof, and a minimum of 4mm thick glass windows and acoustically rated seals.

Category 2 – Reduction of 30-45 decibels, applies to floors, entry doors, external walls, roof, and a minimum of 10.38mm thick laminated glass windows and full perimeter acoustically rated seals.

Category 3 – Reduction of 35-47 decibels, applies to floors, entry doors, external walls, roof, and a minimum of 14.38mm thick laminated glass windows and full perimeter acoustically rated seals.

Category 4 – Reduction of 40-52 decibels, applies to floors, entry doors, external walls, roof, and double glazing consisting of two panes of a minimum 5mm thick glass with at least 100mm air gap and full perimeter acoustically rated seals.

Fact Sheet

Solar Power

PLAN, DECIDE, ACTION

Connecting a solar PV (photovoltaic) system is becoming very popular with new home buyers. With the rising cost of electricity, we are all looking at ways to manage that cost. A solar PV system will do just that.

Solar PV is a technology that converts sunlight into direct current electricity by using semiconductors. Put simply, when the sun hits the semiconductor within the PV cell, electrons are freed and form an electric current.

The installation of a solar PV System will achieve two broad objectives:

1. Reduce your electricity costs.
2. Reduce your carbon footprint.

How long will it take for the system to pay for itself?

This is a difficult question to answer as we all have different sized families, different usage and different "power guzzlers" (e.g., a second fridge in the garage, a swimming pool, clothes dryer usage and air conditioner usage).

However, speaking broadly, a realistic term would be three to five years. At that point, the power savings you've made will have paid for the initial outlay and from then on, all savings go directly into your pocket! My personal experience over the past three years has been a 40% to 45% saving on my power bill.

How do I generate the electricity savings?

Your solar PV system will produce electricity, free from the sun, clearly, only while the sun is out.

- <u>During the day,</u> the power from the sun generates electricity to be used during the day.
- <u>At night,</u> you draw your electricity from the grid (at your cost).

If you don't use the electricity generated from the sun during the day, your electricity provider buys your solar generated electricity back from you for a nominal fee. This will be shown on your electricity bill.

What do I need in a solar PV system?

It's very simple … solar panels are mounted on the roof and an inverter (usually mounted in the garage) – and that's it!

In terms of system size, there's no one answer, depending on how many people live in your home and your current power usage. They typically start at 3kw and can run to 12kw; the most common size is 5kw to 6kw.

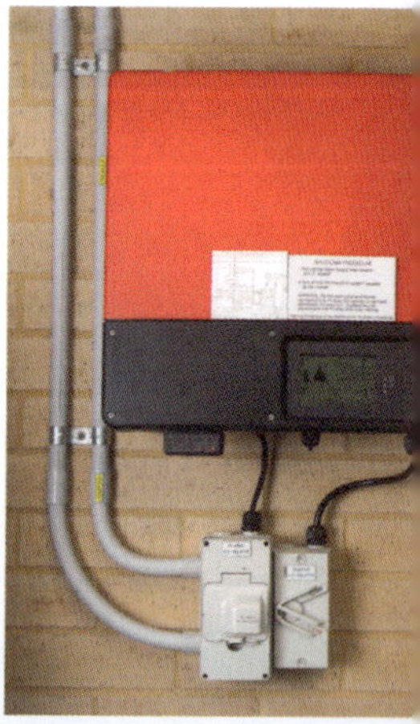

What's next with solar PV Systems?

The next step in the solar evolution is battery storage! So, when the solar system is generating electricity during the day, if there's no one there to use it, it gets stored in a battery for use later, e.g., at night. Sounds great; the only problem is the price.

At the time of writing, a 6.5kw battery storage costs around $12,000 to $16,000 to purchase and you will need a different battery ready Inverter. This price will come down in time, just like VCR recorders in the 1980s!

This industry is one of the most rapidly changing parts of a new home. Speak to your builder and even the system providers to ensure you are up to date with what's available now and what's expected to come in the near future.

As an example, solar roofing is very close to hitting the domestic market. This means that, instead of having the "not so pretty" bulky solar panels all over your roof, the actual tile or roof panel will form your solar panel. Solar glass is also being worked on at the moment.

Just a word of warning, check your objectives for installing solar PV in the first place; if it's just to save money on your power costs, do the maths on the new technology as it comes to market. Work out what your annual electricity bill is and the savings you will make by taking "solar action", then equate it to how long before you will break even on your initial outlay.

Fact Sheet

Air Conditioning

PLAN, DECIDE, ACTION

The best and most efficient time to install air conditioning systems is when your home is being built. Having said that, air conditioning can be installed after you move into the home, if the budget doesn't allow for it now. It's just a bit more inconvenient.

What are my choices?

It falls into one of two categories – **split systems** or **ducted**.

Split system air conditioning

This is an extremely efficient system to run and is an excellent system if you only want to cool/heat up to three to four rooms. After this point, it's more cost efficient to install a ducted system.

Remember, for every split system wall unit you have inside, it will need a compressor unit mounted on the outside of your home; too many of them can become a bit unsightly.

Capacity wise, they run in several sizes, 2.5kw (bedrooms), 3.5kw, 5kw, and 7.1kw (for open plan areas). Price wise, allow from around $2,000 to $3,500 per unit and this is supplied and installed. Each split system comes with its own remote control unit.

Ducted air conditioning

If the budget allows it, this is the way to go. It does everything the split systems do but allows you to provide cooling/heating to the **whole home**. The outlets are **more discreet** and are mounted on the ceiling of the room you are providing air conditioning to. You will **only have one motor** mounted on the outside of your home and **one central wall mounted remote control**, allowing you

Left: Ducted Air Conditioning
Above: Split System Air Conditioning

to determine what rooms are turned on and off at any one time and giving you control of the temperature.

Some of the upgraded remote control units come with a downloadable app to your phone, meaning you can control it from anywhere in the world (as long as you have internet connection). This can be handy if you turn your system on when you leave work on a hot sticky afternoon and your home will be cool by the time you arrive!

Capacity wise, you have plenty of choice and your system will be matched up with the total living area of your home, so it fits each home perfectly.

You have probably heard the term **"reverse cycle"** applied to air conditioners, this means the system can provide both heating and cooling, making their usage all year round. This applies to both split systems and ducted air conditioners.

Fact Sheet

Hot Water Systems

PLAN, DECIDE, ACTION

This is a very important choice to be made, as we have all experienced an unreliable hot water system of some type, at some time. You want your hot water to be consistent, reliable, and efficient to run. So, here are your choices:

Electric

Available in a range of sizes, usually installed on the outside of the home and are limited by the amount of water your system holds. Once it runs out – you're on cold water! When electric systems are used in combination with solar PV systems, this can be a fair option.

Heat pump

This system uses heat from the air to produce hot water, available in a range of sizes. This is a good system but is expensive to purchase, around $3,000 to $3,500.

Heat Pump Hot Water System

Solar

The traditional roof mounted system with the water storage and solar panels all on the roof and fairly visible.

Solar split system with electric boost

This system has two solar panels mounted on the roof and the hot water is stored outside in a cylinder storage unit. It comes with an electric boost if the solar has run out.

Above Left: Solar Hot Water Sysyem
Above Right: Solar Hot Water System with Electric Boost
Left: Gas Hot Water System

Solar split system with gas boost

Same system as the electric boost above but uses a gas boost instead of electric. This gives it the added advantage of providing continuous hot water.

Gas

Gas would be the pick of the bunch for several reasons, very inexpensive to buy and set up, very good value to run, never run out of hot water and can even plumb your BBQ up directly. It only takes up a small space on the external wall and can even be semi-recessed into the wall for neatness. Whether you are using natural gas or on site cylinder gas, the above principles still apply.

PART III

The Construction Process

THE BUILD BEGINS

Now let's look at the construction process, once building approvals have been granted. Typically, the building part of the construction process will take 3 to 4 months:

APPROVALS RECEIVED FROM COUNCIL!

1 Week

- **Builder on site**
- **Construction commenced**

1 Week

- **Slab in the ground – 15% Payment**

1 Week

- **Frame up – 20% Payment**

1 Week

- **Roof on – 15% Payment**

5 Weeks

- **Enclosed (Lock Up) – 20% Payment**

3 Weeks

- **Fixing – 20% Payment**

3 Weeks

- **Practical Completion – 5% Payment**

1 Week

HANDOVER!

NOTE: 5% deposit is paid at contract signing

Fact Sheet

Home Sewage Treatment Plant (HSTP)

If your estate doesn't have town sewerage available (and 95% of the blocks that are 2,000m2 plus won't have it) you will need to include a HSTP. This will usually take the form of a 9,000 litre to 10,000 litre concrete in ground tank. Make sure the manufacturer your builder uses produces purpose-built tanks, moulded as a one-piece unit, eliminating joins and offer at least a 15-year warranty. The concrete tank should have steel reinforcement as part of its construction.

Your tank should have two alarms:

One audible and one visual alarm, to alert you to any problem with the operation of your HSTP.

How does it work?

A quality HSTP system is one of the best forms of recycling in your home. In simple terms, all the waste from the toilets and the "grey" water (from basins, sinks, showers, etc.) is moved to the pre-treatment chamber of the HSTP tank. This happens via gravity, from your home to the tank, so correct plumbing and installation of the tank is vital. Ensure your builder is experienced with this process.

From there, all waste is moved into the secondary pre-treatment chamber of the HSTP, while solids are allowed to settle at the bottom for now. Air is introduced via a silent blower and bacteria digest most of the remaining organic material. The liquid then flows into the third clarification chamber and any sludge that remains is returned to the pre-treatment chamber.

The treated effluent then passes through a filter and finally through a chlorinator to kill any viruses that may remain. The treated effluent is then stored in the irrigation chamber until enough levels build up to trigger the submersible irrigation pump via an automatic float switch.

The cycle is complete as the treated effluent is pumped out via an above ground sprinkler into a pre-determined effluent disposal area (see photo to the right).

It's a simple process and you don't do anything different inside your home compared to a town sewered block.

The big advantage is you are re-using your waste water to irrigate the lawn or even gardens, saving on using rain water or town water.
While this treated effluent is 65 times cleaner than septic tank effluent, it is not to be drunk, just used to irrigate.

What size system do I need?

The system described above will cater for up to 10 bedrooms, so it's unlikely you will need anything larger.

What does it cost?

Expect a system like this to cost around $12,000 – supplied, installed, pump, power connected, all plumbing to your home, effluent sprinklers set up, council application and approvals.

Water Tanks

You may need to have water tanks if your block doesn't have access to full pressure town water, although a lot of the acreage estates are now developing their blocks with full pressure town water already supplied.

In the case of not having any town water, you will need to collect all your water from rain on your roof and store it in tanks. The tanks are plumbed up to your home to cater for all your water needs.

What happens if you run out of rain water? – you will have to buy in water, delivered by a truck. Most councils will only require you to have 45,000 litres of water as a minimum, but I would recommend you keep 63,000 litres on hand (this is still only two tanks, both 31,500 litres each, as per photo at right).

What type of tank?

You can choose from concrete in ground water tanks, poly or corrugated steel above ground water tanks. The in ground concrete tanks can be a bit more expensive but not very visible. They are also a natural insulator, keeping the water at a constant cool temperature. The concrete tanks are also fire resistant.

The poly or corrugated steel above ground tanks can be a bit of an eyesore but you can position them out of sight as much as possible. (e.g., behind a shed).

The poly or corrugated steel tanks won't keep the water as cool as the concrete tanks. The poly tanks will burn in the event of a fire. All tank types come with a pump.

Poly rainwater tanks, installed on a concrete base

In the event of power failure, a generator can be plugged into your meter box to provide power to some essential services e.g, pumps on water tanks, refrigeration and limited lighting. Ensure this is set up on your meter box during construction. Even if you have access to town water, you may still choose to install a water tank specifically for irrigation purposes. There are various sizes and shapes available. 5,000 litres to 20,000 litres are the most common sizes for this purpose.

Steel water tanks, above ground

Fact Sheet

Steel Frame versus Timber Frame

This is a question clients regularly ask; their main motivation is usually to avoid any termite damage, which is understandable, as termites are found all around mainland Australia. Here's an overview of the pros and cons of each product.

Steel frame and trusses

PROS

- Termites are unable to cause any damage to the house frame and truss.
- Durability – steel does not warp or expand.
- Steel frames allow for rapid assembly.
- Steel will not rot, won't burn and is highly resistant to fungus.

CONS

- Steel is not energy efficient and conducts heat 400 times faster than wood, reducing insulation properties by around 60%.
- Cost – allow around $8,000 extra for an average 260m2 home.
- Building with steel does require specialised tools and knowledge, a lot of trades won't have these skill levels.
- If termites do get into your steel frame home, they still have a lot of wood to eat, e.g., all architraves, skirting boards, window and door jambs.
- It is more difficult to hang pictures, clothes dryers, big screen TV's on the walls, compared to timber.

Timber frame and trusses

PROS

- Very cost effective compared to steel.
- To avoid warping, ask your builder to use a minimum MGP-10 quality timber.
- All trades are fully conversant in working with timber frames.
- Timber frame structures will achieve a much better thermal performance.
- Timber construction requires less CO2 to process and produce than steel.
- Responsibly sourced wood is renewable, forests will regrow to provide a wide range of other benefits.

CONS

- Will burn in the event of a fire.
- Timber is suspectable to termite attack, if left unprotected.

To summarise

As you can see, both products have their plusses and minuses. Given the additional cost that a steel frame has on your budget, I would always opt for the **treated timber product**. The only disclaimer to be added: make sure the termite system is a tried and tested one. Also, the timber frame and truss doesn't have the high heat conductivity that steel does.

Fact Sheet

Colorbond versus Roof Tiles

THE BUILD BEGINS

Another conundrum clients are faced with is their roof – what is best: colorbond or tiles? Let's have a look at the good and bad points for each option.

Colorbond roofing

PROS

- Colorbond is one of the toughest and most advanced building materials today. It's been tried and tested for over 50 years in some of the harshest environments in Australia.
- Colorbond is corrugated metal with a bonded paint finish that seals it from moisture; it won't absorb water like concrete tiles.
- Colorbond is around 1/10 the weight of tiles, making the truss construction less expensive.
- Metal roofing is 100% recyclable, it's efficient to transport and contributes to less on-site wastage.

- Colorbond requires little to no maintenance; the manufacturer guarantees the product for 25 years.
- Colorbond roofing will usually be around the same price as tiles, sometimes a little less expensive.

CONS

- The colour does deteriorate around the 10-year mark and needs to be refinished, this will depend on the chosen colour; lighter colours are less likely to fade.
- This roofing can be somewhat noisy unless an acoustic blanket is placed down before the roofing is installed; however, some people like the sound of rain on the roof.

Roof tiles

PROS

- Today's roofing titles are mostly made from moulded, tinted concrete and are very durable and long lasting.
- Roofing tiles can come in many shapes: curved, flat, fluted, or interlocking, and in many styles.
- Impervious to rot and insect damage, tiled roofs will never decay.
- Environmentally friendly material; tile roofs are made from earth minerals not chemicals and they can be pulverized and recycled when they are removed.
- Energy efficient; the heavy thermal mass of tiles will help regulate indoor temperatures.

CONS

- Roof framing needs to be very structurally sturdy, in order to support the weight of roof tiles.
- In certain conditions, they can crack or splinter.
- Difficult installation; installing tile roofing requires professional roofing contractors with extensive experience. The tiles will need to be measured, laid in a specific pattern and checked so that no moisture gets through.
- Repairs, when needed, can be expensive, from water blasting dirt to re-pointing the hills on a tiled roof.
- Ensure your builder installs storm seals to the valleys (when using tiles); they must be added to avoid leaking through the roof.

Fact Sheet

Termite Protection

THE BUILD BEGINS

Termites live in the ground and can do serious damage to your home, if left unchecked! Not trying to scare you but they are destructive pests and have been known to destroy the wall and roofing timbers of an unprotected home within 3 months. Termites occur throughout mainland Australia, with an incidence of attack in virtually all urban areas.

Home and building insurance policies will not cover remedial and repair costs of damage caused by termites to structural and decorative timbers in a building.

So now, the good news – here's how you can control them to avoid your home being the next termite meal:

- Ensure your builder is using a reliable, well-known prevention system.
- The best system is a barrier protection around the internal perimeter of your home.
- This physical barrier prevents termites from crossing it and attacking your home.

- Remove all soil and wood contact around the house.
- Remove all timber, wood, plants, mulch and cardboard from around the foundation of your home.
- Make sure your stormwater drains are running away and not pooling near the house.
- Fix leaky taps and avoid all excess moisture around the house.
- Have a licensed pest inspector look over your house every 12 months.
- Look out for signs of "mud packs" – these are the termite transport tunnels.
- Don't forget – termites will not only eat your frame and roof trusses but your architrave and skirting board timber plus the window and door jambs.

The key to successful termite management is to stop them getting into your home in the first place!

Fact Sheet

Cladding

THE BUILD BEGINS

Cladding can achieve a wide variety of looks, from contemporary to traditional, making it ideal for new homes providing an alternative, reinforced material to create an asbestos-free product. It's a non-loadbearing layer attached to the outside of a home to resist water and protect the building from the effects of weather.

Cladding can be made from different materials – weatherboards (made from natural timber products), engineered timber, or fibrous cement (FC Sheeting).

The cladding is screwed or nailed to the house frame via a secret nailing method or with nail heads showing, for authenticity.

Demand for cladding continues to grow in Australia as it provides increased flexibility with designs.

What are the advantages of using fibrous cement cladding?

- It will not burn and is resistant to permanent water damage.
- Termites cannot eat it.
- Resistant to rotting and warping.
- Stylish and versatile.
- Durable and low maintenance.
- Pre-primed product, easy to paint.

What's fibrous cement cladding made of?

- Sand
- Cement
- Water
- Cellulose fibre

Fact Sheet

Insulation/ 6 Star Energy Rating

THE BUILD BEGINS

The Building Code of Queensland requires your builder to achieve a 6 star energy rating for your home to be approved. Most builders will pass on any additional charges to you if the building falls short of this level. Discuss this with your builder before entering into any contracts and ensure they will guarantee a 6 star energy rating at their cost, if required.

All states have a similar energy rating system.

What does a 6 star energy rating mean?

A 6 star energy efficiency rating applies to your home's building envelope – its roof, walls, floor and windows. 6 star requirements also include efficiency standards for lighting but not for plug-in appliances.

6 star homes are projected to use 24 percent less energy through heating and cooling compared to 5 star homes.

What does house energy rating mean?

An energy performance certificate shows the energy current and potential energy rating of a home, known as a 'SAP rating'. SAP stands for Standard Assessment Procedure and is the government's recommended system for producing a home energy rating.

What is the best and most cost effective way of improving a home's energy rating?

There are a number of ways, but the best is insulation and this can take a number of forms. Here's the main ones used in residential housing:

Ceiling insulation

Fibre batts – This product is one of the most popular and comes in a number of ratings. Suggest R2.5 to R3.5 is used, it's made up of very thin glass fibres that are spun like fairy floss to create millions of air pockets. These air pockets are very poor conductors of heat and resist the flow of air or radiation through the insulation.

Features and Benefits:

- Reduces heat in your home
- Improved comfort all year round
- Saves on energy costs
- Non combustible material
- Low allergen

Wall wrap insulation

Wall wraps are pliable building membranes applied to the outside of the building frame. It will reduce the risk of condensation formation which can lead to mould.

Features and Benefits:

- Reduces draughts through the wall frame
- Reduces moisture entry through the walls
- Provides equivalent R1.3 rating protection
- Increases energy efficiency

External wall frame insulation

The fibreglass batt insulation is supplied to fit tightly between standard width studs without the need for on site cutting and is self supporting. An R1.5 rating is fine for 70mm stud walls and can reduce energy used for heating and cooling by up to 20%, leading to a decrease in your energy consumption and ultimately, your energy bills.

Features and Benefits:

- Insulation fits in a single step
- No further attachment method required
- Sized to fit tightly between standard stud centres
- Enhances acoustic performance of walls

Roof insulation – anticon and foil blanket

Anticon is a foil faced insulation blanket specifically designed for temperature and noise control in homes with Colorbond metal roofs. (*Anticon* is short for anti-condensation.)

Features and Benefits:

- Cool in summer, prevents heat loss in winter
- Made from up to 80% recycled content
- Reduces overall energy usage
- Non combustible
- Reduces rain noise

Roof insulation is the most important part of your insulation plan: make sure it's included.

Acoustic Insulation

A soundscreen type of insulation is typically used in internal walls as a high density acoustic insulator to reduce noice transfer between rooms and will assist in creating a quieter home. It is typically used in media rooms, game rooms, home gym rooms and children's retreats.

Features and Benefits:

- Reduce noice transfer between rooms
- Helps isolate rooms for a quieter home
- Limits noise transfer in 2-storey homes
- Non-combustible
- Backed by a 70 year product warranty

Fact Sheet

Driveway Crossovers

THE BUILD BEGINS

A crossover is part of the driveway that goes over an open drainage pipe. (also known as pipe crossings).

- The main purpose for a crossover is to allow any stormwater to flow freely under the driveway and allow ease of access to vehicular traffic to the property.
- Pipe crossings or crossovers are a requirement along the road reserve in properties where a kerb and channel does not exist.
- Your builder is required to apply for and receive approval from the council for the construction of a crossover or pipe crossing driveway.
- However, all maintenance of residential driveways and crossovers and within a resident's own property is the responsibility of the property owner.

Fact Sheet

Construction Loans: How Do They Work?

A construction loan is a mortgage agreement designed specifically for those who are building a new home.

With a construction loan, the lender releases funds as building progress is made. The lender will consider the total amount required to pay the builder to complete the construction.

This amount is then broken down into "progress payments". These payments come out of your mortgage fund and are made as each stage of the construction is reached. One big advantage here is you only pay interest on the amount drawn down.

Here's a few things that a lot of people don't understand about construction loans:

1. You don't need to already own land!

It's normal to have construction loans for people that include both the home and the land; it's all part of the cost of building a new home. If you already have your land, that's great, but you don't need to.

2. Once you have a loan approval, don't go on a spending spree!

Sometimes people think "Great, I'm qualified for a huge loan" and they go out and buy a new car! This can be a big problem as it changes your ratio of income to debt, which means you may not get approved for the construction loan that is needed to complete the payment for your new home.

3. Don't forget to pay your other bills!

This one may seem obvious, but things happen sometimes that might have a bigger impact than you think. The truth is your lender does not care what the reason is you're late in paying your electricity bill; this type of activity can have a big impact on your credit score.

4. Make sure you have a contingency plan

There will always be some unplanned expense that arises when building a new home. It may be your soil type coming back higher than was expected, you may hit rock when the house pad is being cut … So, these and other self-inflicted expenses (upgrading your oven to the latest Euro model!) can and will happen. Make sure you have some extra money set aside to ensure the construction can keep moving along.

How much is enough? Talk to your builder about potential "construction" items that may happen (soil type, rock, retaining walls, etc); they will give you a realistic amount. For your own possible upgrades, a good idea is to have around $10,000 put aside for lawns and landscaping. If you need to dip into these funds along the way, it's your choice – the landscaping may have to wait another six months or so!

Fact Sheet

Home Warranty Insurance

THE BUILD BEGINS

Most residential building work done in Queensland valued at over $3,300 (including labour and materials) must have home warranty insurance. As part of the building process, your builder pays a premium to the QLD Building and Construction Commission (QBCC) to insure the construction. This amount is included as part of your contract and is paid before any work can begin.

It may protect you when:

- A licenced builder does not complete the contracted residential construction and you have terminated the building contract.
- The contractor fails to rectify defective work.
- The building suffers from subsidence or settlement.
- If the QBCC pay out on a claim, the builder is pursued to recover the claimed amount.

Make sure you have a contract

It's important you have a signed contract with your builder and make sure that builder is licenced. Apart from being a legal requirement, it ensures that you have access to the full range of benefits under the home warranty scheme.

How long does a home warranty last?

The work is covered for a period of six years and six months from the date on whichever of the following comes first:

- The premium is paid by the builder on behalf of the owner.
- A contract is entered into by both parties.
- Work is commenced.

Checking for insurance cover

If you have signed a building contract for residential construction work, the QBCC will send you a certificate of insurance. This can always be checked by contacting the QBCC with the property lot number, address, and plan number.

About the Author

I'm honoured to have the opportunity to put onto paper the direct learnings I've had over the past seven years working in the new home building industry as Sales Manager, with most of that time for Stroud Homes Brisbane South.

I hope the various topics covered in this book will demystify the process of building a new home. During this process, you are exposed to a range of emotions your clients go through, including some stressful times and happy times, and you realise and remind yourself you are not dealing with just the sale of a commodity here, but the sale of someone's own home!

Knowledge in any endeavour will lead to confidence in the challenge that lies ahead.

I've worked in sales roles for 45 years, since starting as a shop assistant with Woolworths Variety Stores at the age of 15. I've been fortunate enough to have worked in a variety of industries, but without a doubt, I've enjoyed the new home building Sales Manager role the most. To have the opportunity to work with clients on their new home dream right from the early planning to actually handing them a set of keys to their brand new home is incredibly satisfying.

The new home building industry is one that demands long hours, an "always available" attitude, and the willingness to sacrifice Saturdays and Sundays. I must acknowledge the support and understanding of my family, including my wife, three children and seven grandchildren, as I haven't been available for birthdays and special occasions as much as I would have liked. It would be impossible to take on this role without their support.

Printed in Dunstable, United Kingdom

91218512R00042